# Old Dundonald

Alex F. Young

Dundonald Castle in the Edwardian period, the hillside under the west wall littered with a children's outing. The hill's earliest crown may have been a timber and earth hill fort, lost to a fire around 1000 AD. Today's stone castle may have been built in 1371 to celebrate the accession of King Robert II (1326-1390) – the first Stewart monarch – and grandson of Robert Bruce. Between the window on the right and a matching one on the east side, would have been the main hall. The extension to the right was a later addition.

First published in the United Kingdom, 2018,
by Stenlake Publishing Ltd.
Telephone: 01290 551122
www.stenlake.co.uk

ISBN 9781840337969

Printed by Berforts, 17 Burgess Road, Hastings, TN35 4NR



## Acknowledgements

Mehzebin Adam of the British Red Cross, Dr. Kirsteen Croll (Friends of Dundonald Castle), Elaine Grant, Anne Fitzgerald, Anne V Kerr, David Knox, Sandra & John Liquorish, Irene McMillan (Dundonald Historical and Archive Society), Jim McQuiston, James Picken, Colin Taylor, Andrew Vernon and, David and Anne Watts.

## Illustration Acknowledgements

Dundonald Historical and Archive Society: front cover, inside back cover, 5, 6, 12, 13, 18, 20, 29, 30, 33; Hillhouse Quarry Group: 47, 48; John R Hume: inside front cover, 16, 17, 19, 21, 27; Friends of Dundonald Castle: 1.

## Bibliography

*The New Statistical Account of Scotland*, vol. 5, Ayr–Bute, *Parish of Dundonald*, The Rev. Alexander Willison, pub. William Blackwood & Sons, Edinburgh, 1845.

James H Gillespie, *Dundonald: A Contribution to Parochial History*, pub. John Wylie & Co., Glasgow, 1939.

Francis H Groome, *Ordnance Gazetteer of Scotland*, Thos. C. Jack, Grange Publishing Works, Edinburgh, 1885.

Robert Paton Harvie, *John Harvie (1730-1822) of Newport, Nova Scotia: Three Generations of Descendants, The Nova Scotia Historical Quarterly*, vol. 6, no. 4, 1976.

Alexander Hastie Millar, *The Castles and Mansions of Ayrshire, Illustrated in Seventy Views*, pub. William Paterson, Edinburgh, 1885.

James Paterson, *County of Ay: With a Genealogical Account of the Families of Ayrshire, vol. I*, pub. Thomas George Stevenson, Edinburgh, 1847.

James Paterson: *County of Ayr: With a Genealogical Account of the Families of Ayrshire, vol. II*, pub. Thomas George Stevenson, Edinburgh, 1852.

*Dundonald Castle – Official Guide*, Historic Scotland, Longmore House, Salisbury Place, Edinburgh.

# Introduction

Hamlets, villages and towns grew from a seed in the fertile ground around an ancient point, which in Dundonald's case was not its 12th-13th century castle, as might be expected, but the church on the high ground to the south. Main Street was the road from Dreghorn in the north through the village and Bogend Toll to Tarbolton in the south, with a branch road to Loans. Coming through Gatehead, the road from Kilmarnock joined Main Street opposite the castle until 1928-29 and the opening of the bypass road. Built under the guidance of the Board of Agriculture for Scotland, the new road ran from west of Boghead, skirted the south side of Palmer Mount (a large circular plantation of trees – now (2018) Palmermount Industrial Estate), and formed a crossroads with the Dreghorn road, creating twelve smallholdings by its sides.

The houses on Main Street were of little significance compared to the parish, a seven mile sided equilateral triangle with the coast from Irvine Harbour to the Pow Burn on the west, and the River Irvine to the north. In 1755 the parish had a population of 983 which by 1831 had grown to 5,579. The census a decade later shows Dundonald had 345 inhabitants (2016 estimate – 2,660) whilst Troon's developing harbour had increased its figure to 1,409 (2016 estimate – 14,530).

By the mid 1850s the west side of Main Street, from Winhouse Yett to the church, was built, and on the east from the Tarbolton Road to what is now Richmond Terrace had been completed. According to the 1855 Ordnance Survey Book – *the dwellings are indifferent and chiefly occupied by labouring people.*

With no major industries – Monsanto arrived in 1964 and departed in 1979 – employment centred on the land, the railway and the quarries, and hence housing development was slow. Ayr County Council started in the 1920s, but only after the Second World War did council house building gather pace, leading to private sector house building programmes.

The photo above shows the steps from Winhouse Yett, leading up to the castle, grazing cattle and sheep keeping the grass, and the trees and shrubs, trimmed. Around 1953 the castle and its grounds were taken over by Ayr County Council, the castle later passing to Historic Scotland. In 1986, with the fabric made safe, the public were given access, but in 1995 South Ayrshire Council found some money and the visitor centre was built. Opened in 1998, it is run by Friends of Dundonald Castle.

The east wall, with the window to the hall on the left and an entry to the right with the chapel window above.

Winhouse Yett cottages, on Auchans estate, were demolished in 1914 leaving the name to the road leading to the castle. The valuation roll has variants of the name – 1855-1875: Windhouse Yett: 1885-1925; Winhouse Yett, and from 1929, Winehouse Yett. Despite the romance of it being the route of contraband wine from the coast in smuggling days, its root may be more prosaic, deriving from *windhouse* or windmill and *yett*, 'a natural pass between hills'. Neighbouring Monkton had its windmill, later a dovecot, and Ballantrae lies under the shadow of another, both shown on Armstrong's 1775 map of Ayrshire.

Mrs. James Baird Thorneycroft of Hillhouse – Annie Chalmers Nicol (1857-1934) who had married Thorneycroft in 1885 – with Lady Sophia Constance Allenby Montgomerie (1863-1942), daughter and heir to the 14th Earl of Eglinton (Archibald William Montgomerie), to the right, preparing to throw the first jack to open the Montgomerie Bowling Club's 1913-14 season, the last on the three rink green to the south of Winhouse Cottages. A year later the club would be on its new green, to the north of the cottages, and the Rev. James Hogg Gillespie, standing to the left, would be watching his new houses rise.

The four houses to the left of the bowling green, in Winhouse Yett and Main Street, appear in the Valuation Roll for 1914-1915 as the property of the Rev. James H Gillespie and *in course of erection*. The following year, their occupants were (from the left): The Nursing Association, per Miss Brownlie, Secretary; Charles Stevenson, residenter; Jeannie Gilchrist, spinster, and William Davidson, joiner. With the benefit of his deceased father's estate (Andrew Gillespie, d. 1912), the Rev. Gillespie had bought the land (with the original bowling green), demolished the cottages, and become a man of property. He later sold the houses.

The war memorial on the Drybridge Road / Kilmarnock Road corner – a Celtic cross of Creetown granite, mounted on a cairn of local whinstone – was manufactured by the sculptors Messrs. Scott & Rae of Eglinton Toll, Glasgow, to a design by Laura Jane Loudon, an art teacher from Ayr, and unveiled on Sunday 9th January 1921. Despite the exceptional wind and rain, St. Giles Church was filled for the service and the memorial address by Lieut. Gen. Sir Aylmer Gould Hunter-Weston (1864-1940), who had served at Gallipoli and the early stages of the Battle of the Somme, but was now MP for Bute and North Ayrshire (1918-1935). As part of the service, conducted by the Rev. James Gillespie and the Rev. William Scott of the Free Church, the 54 names on the memorial were read out. The 55th name, Pte (not Drummer) George Mitchell, Black Watch, was added after his death, due to wounds, at Coldstream, Berwickshire, on 17th February 1924. His brother, Joseph Mitchell (killed at Loos on 26th December 1916) is also there. Emerging into driving rain, a pipe band led almost 100 ex-servicemen, the Boys Brigade, the Girl Guides and parishioners to the memorial where, after a few words, the draped Union Flag was removed and *The Last Post* sounded. The 22 parishioners lost in the Second World War are commemorated on plaques within St. Giles Church. In 2014, with a grant of £8,050 from the Centenary Memorials Restoration Fund, the memorial site was renovated and new seating and lighting installed.

The bowling club's pavilion on a 1920s winter's day. When the three rink green to the south of Winehouse Yett cottages proved insufficient to meet growing interest in the sport, Lady Sophia Montgomerie granted land for this new green and clubhouse – on a rent of 1/- per annum. The necessary £600 was raised and the Kilmarnock architect Gabriel Andrew (1851-1933) commissioned to draw plans for the clubhouse. The mason David Richardson of Dreghorn and the village joiner James Murray, made the drawing a reality, and Robert Provand & Son of Rutherglen supplied, and laid, the green. It was opened by Lady Sophia on Saturday 9th May 1914. In 1978 with the title deeds in their own name, Montgomerie Bowling Club became Dundonald Bowling Club and the following year the clubhouse was extended.

Montgomerie Bowling Club and Winehouse Yett, from Castle Hill in the 1920s. Through the canopy of the tree, the war memorial, and the school on Kilmarnock Road, are just visible.

The north end of Main Street from Castle Hill, around 1910, with Gulliland Farm in the middle distance.

By the late 1960s, Kilmarnock Road was flanked with housing – Bruce Avenue on the right, and Fullarton Avenue on the left.

With four classrooms and capacity for 260 pupil, the school was built to plans by the Kilmarnock architect Thomas Smellie (1860-1938), replacing the 1802 built Montgomerie Hall. The work was financed by the school board through a public loan of £2,500 – to be repaid in 30 years – but trimming two classrooms from Smellie's plan saved £600. Supervised by the contractor, Messrs Orr, McLean & Company of Troon, the foundation stone was laid by Lady Sophia Montgomerie on Saturday 5th October 1895. The following year, the teacher's house, to the left in the photograph, was built for Hugh Gibb. Born in Kilmarnock in 1857, Gibb spent his working life in Dundonald, retiring to Troon, with his wife Isabella *née* Robertson, having married in 1882. She died in 1928 and he in 1933, both at 34 Harling Drive.

In this group of 13-14 year old boys at the school around 1912, only one is identifiable – James McQuiston (b.1898), seated second from the right in the middle row. His parents, Hugh McQuiston and Janet *née* Watson had married at Stair, Ayrshire in 1877 and Hugh, an electrical engineer, now cared for the generator at Dankeith House. James was apprenticed to the joiner and cartwright, James Murray, and served as a wheelwright with the Royal Artillery at Woolwich during the First World War. In 1925 he married Mary Crawford Turnbull, a maid at Dankeith House, in her home village, New Cumnock. In the late 1930s he worked at Hillhouse Quarry, as a joiner, and ended his days in Dundonald in 1991.

The ground for the three public and three bedroom house Redholme, on the Kilmarnock Road–Main Street corner, was bought from Eglinton Estate in 1895 by Dr. John MacDowal Smith and his wife, Isabella Thornton, who had married at Edinburgh the previous year. A native of Perth, Smith graduated from Glasgow University with a Bachelor of Medicine degree in 1879 and served as a doctor in Glasgow, Patna, Alyth, Davidson's Mains and West Calder before coming to Dundonald and the new house around 1900. Three years later they left for Cheltenham, where he died in 1905, Isabella dying at Newlands, Glasgow in 1937. Redholme was rented for many years before being sold.

Today's (2018) premises The Oaks, veterinary centre, was in the early 1920s providing refreshments for cyclists, and the red sandstone cottage is now the Dundonald branch of Newfield Pharmacy. The straw on the footpath outside what is now the Keystore would have been for William Boyd, the carter, whose yard and stabling was to the rear.

The west side of Main Street in March 1988 when the premises at No. 22 were occupied by John Allan, the electrician, of Darvel. In July 1991, with the business gone, South Ayrshire Council granted planning permission to convert the shop to a living room within the house.

Of the two shops opposite Richmond Terrace – the general store of Cowley & Wilson and Jenni-F the hairdresser – only the general store, photographed in 1989, remains. Amedeo Guidi ran it as a chip shop / confectioners until his death in 1924 when his widow Mary, *née* Woods, rented it to a succession of tenants. Arthur Cowley (d.2017) was a Civil Aviation Authority air traffic controller until the early 1970s when he bought the premises and became a general store proprietor – living above the business. His partner, Wilson, dropped out early. In 2012 the shop became a Premier Store with a new owner.

Captain Johanne Picken, with Janice McFarlane to the right, leading the 1st Dundonald Girl Guides past Richmond Terrace in a parade along Main Street around 1960. Founded in 1910 by Agnes Baden-Powell – her brother, Robert, having founded the Boy Scouts – the Guides movement started in Dundonald in April 1918 with a troop of 28 girls, following a public meeting the previous November attended by Miss Loelia Buchan-Hepburn, Deputy Chief Guide for Scotland. The village's interest in guiding waxed and waned over the years, being re-founded in 1953, but is now resting. Johanne came to Dundonald as a four-year-old in 1947 when her father, Robert, took over as postmaster, with the general store. Educated at Dundonald Primary School and Marr College, Troon, she trained at Jordanhill College of Education, Glasgow, and was posted to Kilmarnock's Bentinck Primary School, before moving to Symington Primary School, where she was head teacher until 1995. She died in 2003.

Richmond Terrace, leading to Bruce Avenue, in 1988. It appears on the 1854 Ordnance Survey map (Ayrshire, sheet XXll.7, Dundonald) but it is not known when it was built, or by whom. In the late 1920s Adam Haldane Galbraith Richmond, the gas work manager, bought the nine house terrace and passed it to his sons, David (b.1907) and John Revie Richmond (b.1908), who had it renovated, before occupying two of the houses, John at No. 5 and David at No. 7. From the 1930s it was named Richmond Terrace. The state of disrepair shown in this photograph was corrected in 1990, when the wall to the left was removed.

Matthew Struthers and his wife, Marion, flank their seven year old son, Adam Brownlie Struthers, and an assistant, outside his shop (2018, Totally Pampered) on Main Street, about 1916. Matthew was from Galston, Ayrshire and whilst working as a power-loom tenter, i.e. he cleaned looms and replaced bobbins, at a mill in Strathaven, Lanarkshire he met Marion Brownlie, a weaver, whom he married in June 1905. Pedalling his message bike around the village he yodelled, and on winter evenings taught children to play draughts in the Montgomery Hall. They retired to Darvel, and on his death, aged 81 years, in April 1953, his widow Marion, and son Adam, moved to Cambuslang, where they died – she in 1962 and Adam, unmarried, in 1986. Matthew's brother James (b.1886) and his wife, Jeannie, *née* Gebbie, ran the business for some years.

The Dundonald Inn (the one time Dundonald Hotel) – the 'Top Pub' – in February 1989, on its way to another liquidation, where it arrived in 2004 before rising as the multi-national cuisine restaurant Chef's World Buffet in 2013. The business had a history of problems. In June 1905, William Pollock, hotel-keeper, Dundonald Hotel, appeared before the Sheriff at Ayr and was sequestrated – in June 1912, Robert Bone of the same business, in the same premises, went through the same process. The public notice of the auction in July 1912, at the King's Arms Hotel, Irvine, shows the upset price, including goodwill, was £650. It was bought by Andrew Nimmo who passed the baton to David Bowman in the late 1920s.

Main Street in the 1920s, with the manse gatehouse on the left and, before Struthers' shop on the right, the entry to the gas works. Its earliest notice comes in the 1885 Valuation Roll when the Dundonald Gas Light Company was in the charge of Samuel Dalziel (1829-1904), manager of the Kilmarnock Corporation Gas Company, 16 West Langlands Street, Kilmarnock. By 1901 it was owned by Adam Haldane Galbraith Richmond (1873-1935), gas manufacturer, and native of Whitburn, West Lothian, where his father, John Richmond, had been manager of its gas works. In 1908, George William Anderson and Robert Bruce Anderson, of London, bought the works and renamed the business, Dundonald Gas Company, but despite initial capital of £3,000, their company went into liquidation in 1923, and Adam Richmond returned.

Flanked by mature trees, and crowned by the castle on the hill behind, the manse lodge in 1926, when occupied by Robert Wilson. It dates from the early 1880s, when the Rev. John Sime was minister, and its first occupant was William Paton (1835-1900) a Mauchline-born jobbing gardener and his wife Helen *née* McCubbin (1832-1904) of Dundonald. Its humble, two roomed, accommodation was added to in the 1940s – with a bedroom to the right – and again in the 1950s to the rear. As the Masonic Lodge Burns Dundonald, No. 1759 was not founded until 1985, the masonic 'square and compass' symbol atop the lamp, outside the Castle Hotel, is a mystery.

Main Street on a busy day, with 'mine host' from the Inn out chatting to passers-by. The most striking change to this stretch of the street's frontage is that it is now painted white.

From Kirkstyle, on the east side of Main Street, the building line passes the entry to the Free Church to the four 'Nepus' style buildings which date from the early 19th century.

Forty seven year old James Nisbet, master blacksmith, (on the right) outside his premises (rented from Mrs. Mary Dale Muir of Kelso), off Kirkstyle, and adjacent to the Free Church, in the winter of 1905-06. A native of Symington, where his father, William, was also a blacksmith, he married Mary Dunlop there in 1882. Of their seven children (five boys and two girls), William (b.1884) joined him as an apprentice. James died at Kirkstyle on 9th July 1916 from an apoplexy.

The 1843 'Disruption' within the Church of Scotland – should ministers be appointed by the heritors or by the congregation – spawned the 'The Free Protesting Assembly of the Church of Scotland' or simply, The Free Church, when 474 out of over 1,200 ministers left the established church. Sir John Cunningham of Fairlie was introduced to an assembly of the new church on 26th May 1843, and announced that in Dundonald, that morning he had received the names of 354 adherents to the Free Church – and £200 to build a new church. The church, St. Andrews, (the first 'Free Church' building completed in Ayrshire) held its first service in the November and in 1849 the Rev. David Simpson moved into the new manse. Membership, however, did not come up to Sir John's expectations, having only 165 adherents in 1848. In 1942, on the retiral of the Rev. James H Gillespie and the Rev. William Scott of the Free Church, the congregations united and St. Andrew's became the church hall. The photograph dates from 1989.

The parish church, St. Giles, on the west side of Main Street in the summer of 1908. In 1792 an examination, commissioned by the heritors, found its predecessor so ruinous that a replacement was needed. Eleven years later, at their meeting on 6th January 1803 they resolved to have a new church 'before next winter'. A mason, James Hodge (d.1815), was commissioned and at a cost, including a new perimeter wall, of £1,160, Dundonald had its new church by June 1804. The steeple was completed in 1809 and the entrance porch in 1817.

St. Giles manse (now (2018) Glenfoot House) was re-built in 1784 for the Rev. Robert Duncan (1754-1815) who, the previous year, had succeeded the Rev. Thomas Walker. In his 1793 *Statistical Account* report for the parish, Duncan records that ... *it was built, upon a very neat plan, and was the first in this part of the country, which had slated offices*. Five ministers succeeded Duncan as occupants: John McLeod (1815-1841), Alexander Wilson (1841-1866), John Sime (1866-1904), James H Gillespie (1904-1952) and Archie Beaton (1952-1956). In 1956, when the Rev. Archie Beaton moved to the new built manse at the end of Main Street, the former was sold to a Mr. John Lawson of Westmoor, Kilmarnock, for £5,500 and has now passed through other hands.

The Rev. James Hogg Gillespie and his wife Mary in the south-facing sitting room of the manse, where he also performed marriage ceremonies. Born on 7th June 1867 to Andrew Gillespie (d.1912), iron master, and his wife Barbara *née* Hogg (d.1909), when living at 28 Bellgrove Street, Dennistoun, Glasgow, later moving to nearby Seton Terrace. Educated at Dennistoun Academy (a private school, later acquired by Glasgow School Board and, later still, renamed Whitehill Secondary School), he graduated from Glasgow University with a Master of Arts degree in 1892, and in 1895 gained a Bachelor of Divinity degree. Licensed by the Presbytery of Glasgow, he was appointed assistant to the Rev. John Sime at Dundonald in February 1902, and in the April married 32 year old Mary Muir in the Grand Hotel at Glasgow's Charing Cross. They had five daughters: Marjorie (b.1904), Katherine Barbour (b.1906), Mary Muir (b.1908), Elspeth Taylor (b.1911) and Alison Drysdale (b.1914). The death of his father in February 1912 elevated him to a man of property, starting with the building of the four houses at Winehouse Yett. In 1939 his two volume book *Dundonald: A Contribution to Parochial History* was published by John Wylie & Co. of Glasgow. Mary died in December 1940 and in 1944 he married Jean Lindsay Robertson Campbell, who would survive him. The union of Dundonald's Established Church and the Free Church in June 1942 marked his retiral, and a move to Bearsden, where he died in March 1951. He was buried at Dundonald Cemetery, Shewalton, with Mary and their eldest daughter, Marjorie who passed away in 1976.

The Dundonald branch of the Voluntary Aid Detachment (V.A.D.) in the grounds of the Montgomery Hall, with the church behind, in November 1917. Founded in 1909 by the British Red Cross Society, the V.A.D. provided field, and hospital, nursing services throughout Britain and the Empire and by 1914 had 2,500 detachments with 74,000 nurses, two thirds of whom were women. The organisation's Ayrshire area was formed at a meeting in Troon's Unionist Hall in February 1911, eventually having 48 detachments, of which Dundonald was No. 38, under the chairmanship of the Rev. Mrs Gillespie. None of those photographed appear to have served at the Front, although they may have been at the Dick Institute, Kilmarnock, in its wartime role as a hospital. The medals worn by many of them were awarded for first aid and nursing proficiency. A fund-raising booklet, published in 1918, reports that the ladies of Dundonald knitted 3,486 garments, picked thirteen bags of sphagnum moss (for wound dressings) and raised £368 during the year.

Old Loans Road, coming from the left, merges with Tarbolton Road to form Main Street. In 1956 the manse was built on the land to the left.

Tarbolton Road approaching the junction at Old Loans Road, before rounding right into Main Street, in the early 20th century. Springwell Cottage, The Cottage and Ingleneuk, on the right, balanced the three houses opposite.

Roadend Cottage, Priory Cottage and Parkend Cottage on Tarbolton Road in 1924. They appear on the 1860 Ordnance Survey map, but when they were built cannot be ascertained. The map also shows the milestone on the corner marking five miles from both Kilmarnock and Irvine.

The buildings of the 114 acre Laurieston Farm, on the Tarbolton road, from the Symington road, to the south, with Lochside Farm (part of Newfield estate) in the top right. The photograph dates from around 1914 when Laurieston was part of Auchans estate and tenanted by Jeanie Wylie Smith *née* Allan (1852-1948) who had come here, with her husband John Smith, in 1881. He died in 1887, aged 38 years, leaving Jeanie and their three children: Agnes (b.1883), John (b.1885) and Jessie (b.1886) to the farm. Earlier tenants of the property included Robert Faulds (d.1855) and John McKinnon, before George Smith. Jeanie Smith and her son, John, moved to Kilnford Farm around 1920, and were followed by Hugh Glover. With the break-up of the Montgomerie estate in the 1960s, Laurieston with 3.5 acres, was sold. In plan view, the farm and its buildings today (2018) look much as they do on the Ordnance Survey map of 1854, and also feature on the maps produced for the Military Survey of Scotland (1747-1755) by the chief surveyor, Major-General William Roy (1726-1790).

The children's convalescent home, Dundonald House, on Old Loans Road, in 1902, when those under the dining room window were in the care of the 34 year old, Edinburgh-born, matron, Mary Agnes Barlas. Opened in 1883, the home was managed by a committee chaired by The Honourable Susan Caroline Vernon of Auchans and dedicated to the memory of her 22 year old son, Howe William Leveson Vernon, who had died of typhoid, at Auchans House, in January 1882. Despite ample donations (some £770) to build the house (designed by the architect Allan Stevenson of Ayr), it struggled financially through the years, as children, initially those recuperating from hospital treatment, came and went. At one point annual expenses were £250 on an income of £162. In 1948 it was bought by the Royal Scottish Society for Prevention of Cruelty to Children (now Children 1st) and was a children's home until its closure in November 1981. In 1990 it arose as Dundonald House Nursing Home, specialising in dementia care, and by 2018, three generations of the Kerr family were caring for over 90 residents, the accommodation having expanded over the years.

The lodge to Auchans House, on the Drybridge road, around 1905 when occupied by the estate's coachman, Joseph Richardson. It appears to have been contemporary with the house, and demolished with it.

Hugh Montgomerie, 12th Earl of Eglinton (1739-1819), built Auchans (new) House in his last year, for the estate's factor (possibly Monteaulieu Burgess). By the 1850s it was home to Charles Dalrymple Gairdner (1794-1867), factor to the 13th Earl, Archibald William Montgomery, who had been with the Kilmarnock Banking Company. On the death of the 14th Earl (Archibald William Montgomery) in 1892, Auchans was inherited by his daughter, Lady Sophia Constance (1863-1942) who in 1885 married Samuel Hynman Allenby of Fawley, Hampshire. The couple lived, mainly, at Southannan, Fairlie, Ayrshire and Auchans was let to a succession of tenants, some of their names taken as street names in the future development – The Honourable Greville Richard Vernon (Vernon Place); David M'Farlane Wilson (Wilson Place), manufacturer; Major John Alexander Coats, DFC, (Coats Place). It was also rented to Francis Beattie (1885-1945), Unionist MP for Glasgow's Cathcart (1942-45) and chairman of the bakers, William Beattie Ltd., who was killed in a road accident on the Glasgow road near to Logan's Well in December 1945. Alterations made in 1927 included the replacement of the conservatory with a two-storey bay window. In 1947 the estate was bought by the 13th Earl of Dundonald (Thomas Hesketh Douglas Blair Cochrane) (1886-1958). In 1962, the house – four reception rooms, six bedrooms, two nurseries and staff quarters – and its 68 acres, was on the market, and on its way to today's housing development.

Hillhouse appears on the maps of Scotland prepared by Assistant Quartermaster William Roy between 1747 and 1755, following the Jacobite Rebellion when the dearth of maps had been an embarrassment to the Crown forces. The McKerrell family held the estate from the 14th century but this house, probably, late 18th century, features on Armstrong's map of the 1770s. *The Ordnance Survey Name Book* (1854) describes it as – *A superior dwelling house, the property of Mr Orr temporary occupied by the Lord Provost of Glasgow* (Sir Andrew Orr, Lord Provost of Glasgow, 1854-1857). 'Mr Orr' may not have understood the question or was economical with the truth as the property was owned by William McKerrell (1799-1882), then living in Bath and Orr was the tenant. In the early 1890s Robert Mure McKerrell sold the estate to the iron master James Baird Thorneycroft (1851-1918), then of Nether Place, Mauchline, whose real interest would have been the estate's potential as a quarry. In the 1930s Thorneycroft's trustees sold it to the Vernon family.

The West Gatehouse to Hillhouse Estate in 1913, when occupied by George Bell, the 51 year old butler to the house, his 45 year old wife Elizabeth (married Stewarton, 1892) and their daughters, Isabella Calder Bell (19) and Janet Anderson Bell (17). The previous year, George had been butler to Major James Francis Dalrymple of Dunlop House. Built in 1911, when additions were made to the main house, the gatehouse stood on the south side of the Dundonald to Troon road before its re-alignment, north, due to the expanding quarry.

Built between 1781 and 1787 for Alexander Fairlie of Fairlie (1722-1803), to plans by the Edinburgh architect David Henderson, Fairlie House replaced an early tower house (Little Dreghorn). This photograph dates from the 1880s when the estate was owned by William Cathcart Smith Cunninghame of Robertland, who had married Margaret Fairlie, a sister of Alexander. On 23rd March 1782 John Harvie of Irvine wrote to his brother John, who had emigrated to Nova Scotia some 20 years earlier – *I have as mouch ado as any of this pleas I have a gentlemans hous todo in Dendonald Mr. Alexander Farlie of Farlie, Esq which will take three thousand pounds sterling to finish it and I wrought the last year at it and this year and it will serve the next year too. I have contracted for the finishing of the hous it is thought to be best hou in This country sid. I have 8 men and 2 Sawers emploied at present.* The estate remained with the Cunningham family of Caprington until 1920 when it was bought by Captain Patrick James Crichton Stuart, late of the Grenadier Guards, who died at the house in October 1935, aged 67 years. He has been succeeded by a number of owners over the years.

Elizabeth Bratchie *née* Cunningham (b.1857) outside the lodge to Fairlie House where she and her husband Hugh (b.1861), a labourer and stockman on the estate, lived. They had married at Galston in 1888, when he was a 27 year old coal miner living in Henrietta Street, and she a 28 year old lace darner from Manse Rows, and had four children – Hugh (1890-1972), Mary (1892-1978), Robert (1895-1897) and Jane (1898-1983). Both died in the lodge, Elizabeth on 23rd August 1937, aged 79 years, and Hugh, in his 85th year, on 9th February 1946.

Shown on John Thomson's *Atlas of Scotland* (1828), Caraith Hill – spelling variants over the years include Carreath, Corraith, Curreath – was a roadside farmhouse, to the west of Symington. The Horse Tax Rolls of 1787 show a James and Robert Allison of Corraith, paying 10/- for one horse. John Deans Campbell of Old House of Leog on Lerwick's Commercial Street, bought the property in the early 1840s and, apparently, commissioned the Edinburgh architects William Burn and David Bryce to build a new house. It had four public rooms, twelve bedrooms, two dressing rooms, hot and cold water throughout and ample servant's quarters. Campbell died at Bridge of Allan in September 1868 and was succeeded by his son John Stephen Dean Campbell. He did not live on the estate, and tenant followed tenant, until his death at Clarefoot, Moffat in December 1901, aged 45 years, when it passed into the hands of trustees. It was purchased by Peter Jeffrey Mackie (1855-1924), of White Horse Distillers Ltd., Glasgow who lived at the house, with his wife Jessie Lockett Abercrombie (died at Troon, 1945, aged 80 years) until his death. Their son, Captain James Logan Mackie of the Ayrshire Yeomanry, who should have succeeded him, was killed in action on Zeitoun Ridge on 27th December 1917 and buried at Jerusalem War Cemetery. In 1936 the house was bought by the Scottish Youth Hostel Association and served as a 120 bed hostel until 1960, when Craigweil Hostel (now part of Wellington School), Ayr opened. Corraith was demolished in 1968.

On the south bank of the River Irvine, north-west of Drybridge, Shewalton House was built in 1806 for John Boyle (d.1837), replacing a ruinous square tower. The estate dates to 1473, when Lambert Wallace bound himself to a rent of £3 from John de Fullarton of Fullarton, and it remained with the Wallace family until 1715, when sold to William Boyle, brother of David, 1st Earl of Glasgow, and his successors. In October 1879, whilst owned by Captain David Boyle, Royal Navy, Ardrossan, *The Scotsman* newspaper advertised the house to let. It was lit by gas and capable of accommodating a large family but also ... *situated in the centre of the Eglinton Hunt, with stabling for 9 horses*. William Weir of Kildonan took the tenancy. By the 1890s, perhaps attracted by the coal in the ground, it was owned by James Kenneth, coalmaster, Buckredding, Kilwinning. Later neglect hastened its demolition in the 1950s.

Newfield House in the 1880s when owned by William Finnie, of the coalmasters Alexander Finnie & Sons, Kilmarnock and tenanted by Mrs Jessie Fulton Moffat of Paisley. The 677 acre estate included not only the house and grounds, but the farms; Newfield Mains, Galrigside, Roanhill, Boghead and Peatland which yielded a return of £1,351 per annum. In the 16th century, as Galrigs, it was owned by the Wallace family, then by Captain Lawrence Nugent (d.1763) who married Catherine Kennedy, daughter of Sir Archibald Kennedy of Culzean. Nugent may have built, or added to the original, but is credited with changing the name to Newfield. In 1843 it was bought by James Finnie, on his return from London with a fortune, and passed to his third son William, MP for the northern division of Ayrshire from 1868 to 1874. In 1870, William commissioned the architect John Burnet (1814-1901) of Glasgow to design the house illustrated. It was demolished in 1964.

A 1920s view of Hillhouse Quarry from the top of the finishing crusher with, on the left, the spur railway line (closed 1990s) over the Dundonald to Loans road which carried the crushed whinstone to the Kilmarnock–Troon railway line for distribution. The Hillhouse Quarry Company's operations were begun in 1907 by the ironmaster James Baird Thorneycroft (1851-1918), producing railway track ballast and aggregate for road building. On his death the company was managed by trustees until 1934, when it passed to his niece, Dorothy Inez Elinor Vernon *née* Thorneycroft and hence down her line. Today the Hillhouse Group markets ready-mixed concrete, asphalt, concrete blocks and fulfils road building contracts.

A film crew, possibly from Pathe News (later British Pathe) the newsreel and documentary producer, at Hillhouse Quarry in the 1930s as another 30,000 tons of whinstone comes down. Although widely known as 'whin' – the word deriving from the sound made when struck with a hammer – the stone quarried is Teschenite which forms the Hillhouse Sill, a seam of stone between 45 and 60 metres thick.

A Ruston Bucyrus 100 RB caterpillar track power shovel at the quarry face, loading bogeys on the temporary track, which advanced with the quarry wall. Built at Lincoln, the electric-powered 100 RB weighed 134 tons, had a 32 foot boom and a bucket capacity of 3-4 tons. The photograph dates from the 1930s.